DISCLAIMER

The author Blessing Isaackson and the publishers Fairview Training Ltd have made every effort to ensure that the information, tables, drawings, and diagrams contained in this book are accurate at the time of publication. The book cannot always contain all the information necessary for determining appropriate care and cannot address all individual situations; therefore, anyone using the book must ensure they have the appropriate knowledge and skills to enable suitable interpretation. The author does not guarantee and accepts no legal liability of whatever nature arising from or connected to, the accuracy, reliability, currency, or completeness of the content of this book. Users must always be aware that innovations or alterations after the date of publication may not be incorporated into the content. The author and the publisher Fairview training Ltd assume no responsibility whatsoever for the content of external resources in the text or accompanying online materials.

© **Blessing Isaackson 2024**

All rights reserved. No part of this publication may be reproduced, stored in, or introduced into a retrieval system, or transmitted, in any form or by any means (electronic, mechanical, photocopying, recording, or otherwise) without the prior written permission of the author of this book. The information presented in this book is accurate and current to the best of the authors' knowledge. The authors and publisher, however, make no guarantee as to and assume no responsibility for, the correctness, sufficiency, or completeness of such information or recommendation.

Printing History First Edition 2024

The author welcomes feedback from users of this book. Please email your feedback to bisaackson@gmail.com

The CIP record for this book is available from the British Library.

Paperback ISBN: 978-1-7385061-6-3
Hardcover ISBN: 978-1-7396030-7-6

FORWARD

Fairview Training is committed to providing excellent learning resources to our learners with the aim of assisting them to achieve their qualifications.

This manual has been written with the aim of assisting learners to achieve the award in Education and Training and can be an integral part of their training.

Learners can use this material during the training as a reference even when they have completed the course.

Blessing Isaackson
Managing Director
Fairview Training Ltd

Table of Contents

- INTRODUCTION 6
- STRUCTURE OF THE COURSE 8
- ASSESSMENT - HOW THE AET IS ASSESSED 10
- UNITS OF ASSESSMENT 12
- A TEACHER'S ROLE AND RESPONSIBILITIES IN EDUCATION AND TRAINING 14
- THE TEACHING CYCLE 17
- PLANNING AND DESIGN 24
- DELIVERING THE COURSE 30
- LEGISLATION, REGULATORY REQUIREMENTS, AND CODES OF PRACTICE 32
- REGULATORY REQUIREMENTS 34
- WAYS TO PROMOTE EQUALITY AND DIVERSITY 36
- IDENTIFYING AND MEETING INDIVIDUAL LEARNER NEEDS 39
- UNDERSTAND WAYS TO MAINTAIN A SAFE AND SUPPORTIVE LEARNING ENVIRONMENT 44
- GROUP LEARNING NEEDS 46
- BOUNDARIES BETWEEN THE TEACHING ROLE AND OTHER PROFESSIONAL ROLES .. 49
- POINTS OF REFERRAL TO MEET THE INDIVIDUAL NEEDS OF LEARNERS 51
- UNDERSTANDING AND USING INCLUSIVE TEACHING AND LEARNING APPROACHES IN EDUCATION AND TRAINING 54
- PROVIDING DEVELOPMENT OPPORTUNITIES [ENGLISH, MATHEMATICS, AND ICT] 56
- PLANNING AN INCLUSIVE TEACHING AND LEARNING 57
- TEACHING AND LEARNING APPROACH 61
- SELECTING TEACHING AND LEARNING RESOURCES 62
- SELECTING TEACHING AND LEARNING ASSESSMENT METHODS 63
- ENGAGING AND MOTIVATING LEARNERS 65
- PLANNING AN INCLUSIVE TEACHING AND LEARNING 67
- KOLB'S EXPERIENTIAL LEARNING THEORY/LEARNING STYLE MODEL 71
- GROUP C UNDERSTANDING ASSESSMENT IN EDUCATION AND TRAINING 82
- THE PURPOSES OF TYPES OF ASSESSMENT USED IN EDUCATION AND TRAINING 85
- CHARACTERISTICS OF DIFFERENT METHODS OF ASSESSMENT IN EDUCATION AND TRAINING 87
- COMPARE THE STRENGTHS AND LIMITATIONS OF DIFFERENT ASSESSMENT METHODS IN RELATION TO MEETING INDIVIDUAL LEARNER NEEDS 88
- ADAPTING THE ASSESSMENT METHODS TO MEET THE NEEDS OF THE LEARNERS 89
- EXPLAIN WHY IT IS IMPORTANT TO INVOLVE LEARNERS AND OTHERS IN THE ASSESSMENT PROCESS 90
- HOW TO INVOLVE LEARNERS AND OTHERS IN THE ASSESSMENT PROCESS 91

- PEOPLE THAT MAY BE INVOLVED IN THE 92
- ASSESSMENT PROCESS 92
- EXPLAIN THE ROLE AND USE OF PEER AND SELF-ASSESSMENT IN THE ASSESSMENT PROCESS 93
- WHAT IS FEEDBACK? 94
- IDENTIFY SOURCES OF INFORMATION THAT SHOULD BE MADE AVAILABLE TO LEARNERS AND OTHERS INVOLVED IN THE ASSESSMENT PROCESS 96
- EXPLAIN THE NEED FOR KEEPING RECORDS OF ASSESSMENT OF LEARNING 97
- SUMMARISE THE REQUIREMENTS FOR KEEPING RECORDS OF ASSESSMENT IN AN ORGANISATION 98
- OTHER BENEFITS OF RECORD KEEPING 99

INTRODUCTION

The award in Education and Training is an introduction to teaching to all those intending to teach in further education, colleges, independent training, and local authorities.

- It is an important training resource for those not currently teaching or training.
- Those who are currently training and teaching.
- Individuals working as assessors who want to also become trainers or teachers.

WHAT IS INCLUDED IN THIS RESOURCE

This publication covers the learning outcomes of the award in Education and Training:

The learning outcomes are:

- Understanding the roles and responsibilities and relationships in education and training
- Understanding and using inclusive teaching and learning approaches in education and training
- Understanding assessment in education and training.

ENTRY REQUIREMENTS

The qualification is suitable for learners of 19 years of age and above. There are no specific entry requirements and learners do not need to have teaching practice hours to achieve the qualification. There may be a requirement, by a learner's employer for them to hold a current CRB Certificate if they currently or intend to work with learners who are covered by the CRB regulations. It is the learner's responsibility to seek advice from their employer regarding this, along with attending any necessary Safeguarding information events.

PROGRESSION

Successful learners can progress to other teaching, training, assessment, and internal quality assurance qualifications such as:

- Level 4 Certificate in Education and Training
- Level 5 Diploma in Education and Training
- Level 3 Award in Understanding the Principles and Practices of Assessment
- Level 3 Award in Assessing Competence in the Work Environment
- Level 3 Award in Assessing Vocationally Related Achievement
- Level 3 Certificate in Assessing Vocational Achievement
- Level 4 Award in Understanding the Internal Quality Assurance of Assessment Processes and Practice
- Level 4 Award in the Internal Quality Assurance of Assessment Processes and Practice
- Level 4 Certificate in Leading the Internal Quality Assurance of Assessment Processes and Practice
- Level 4 Award in Learning and Development
- Level 4 Diploma in Learning and Development

STRUCTURE OF THE COURSE

Structure Learners must achieve a minimum of 12 credits from three mandatory unit groups.

Group A is mandatory; Groups B and C contain optional units, some of which are taken from the Learning and Development qualification.

Group A - 3 credits.

Group B – a minimum of 6 credits.

Group C – a minimum of 3 credits.

	Units	Unit no	Level	Guided learning hours	Credit Value
	Group A				
1	Understanding roles, responsibilities, and relationships in education and training		3	12	3

Group B

Group B (6 credits from this group

2	Understanding and using inclusive learning and teaching approaches in education and training		3	24	6
3	Facilitate learning and development for individuals (Learning and Development unit)		3	25	6
4	Facilitate learning and development in groups (Learning and Development unit)		3	25	6

Group C

(3 credits from this group)

5	Understanding assessment in education and training		3	12	3
6	Understanding the principles and practices of assessment (Learning and Development unit)		3	24	3

ASSESSMENT - HOW THE AET IS ASSESSED

The award in Training and Education is assessed by the learner compiling a portfolio of evidence.

The micro-teach session and teaching practice

Learners must be involved in at least one hour of microteaching. Each learner must deliver at least one 15-minute microteaching session, which is observed and assessed by a trainer/assessor. For the additional 45 minutes, learners can either deliver additional microteaching sessions or observe the microteaching sessions of other learners. Learners can deliver a one-to-one training session, providing they meet the requirements of the qualification. There is no requirement for learners to use an icebreaker, agree with ground rules, or embed English, maths, and ICT during their micro-teach session. Teaching practice must be observed and assessed by a trainer/assessor using inclusive Teaching and Learning Approaches in Education and Training. Skype or other live media can be used in circumstances where the observer and learner cannot be present in the same room. The observer must check the identification of the learner prior to their delivery. Technical support should be available in case of any problems. It is good practice to visually record the micro-teach session for learners to view in their own time to aid the self-evaluation process, however, this is not mandatory. The sessions can also be viewed by the IQA and EQA to aid the quality assurance process. Learners who are currently teaching or training can be observed and assessed with their own learners in their place of work, instead of being involved with the micro teach sessions. If this is the case, the practice must total one hour.

The micro teach session must be observed and assessed by a member of the delivery/assessment team, appointed by the approved centre. If learners are taking either of the units from the Learning and Development qualification, they must undertake practice and be observed and assessed by a member of the centre staff team, in their place of work, for the following units:

- Facilitate learning and development for individuals.

- Facilitate learning and development in groups.

There is no minimum number of hours of practice, but it should be in the appropriate context with either groups of learners, or individual learners. Training providers must design and use suitable observation and feedback forms that address the criteria of the units.

Course Delivery

Pre-Course Information

All learners should be given appropriate pre-course information regarding any awarding body qualifications. The information should explain the qualification, the fee, the form of the assessment, and any entry requirements or resources needed to undertake the qualification.

Initial Assessment

Training providers should ensure that any learner registered on an awarding body's qualification undertakes some form of initial assessment. The initial assessment should be used to inform a teacher/trainer of the level of the learner's current knowledge and/or skills. Initial assessment can be undertaken by a teacher/trainer in any form suitable for the qualification to be undertaken by the learner/s. It is the training provider's responsibility to make available forms of initial assessment that are valid, applicable, and relevant to the awarding body's qualifications.

UNITS OF ASSESSMENT

Unit 1

Title:	Understanding roles, responsibilities and relationships in education and training
Level:	3
Credit Value	3
Guided learning hours:	12
Learning outcomes The learner will:	**Assessment criteria** The learner can:
1. Understand the teaching role and responsibilities in education and training.	1.1 Explain the teaching role and responsibilities in education and training.
	1.2 Summarise key aspects of legislation, regulatory requirements and codes of practice relating to your own role and responsibilities.
	1.3 Explain ways to promote equality and value diversity
	1.4 Explain why it is important to identify and meet individual learner needs

2. Understand ways to maintain a safe and supportive learning environment	2.1	Explain ways to maintain a safe and supportive learning environment.
	2.2	Explain why it is important to promote appropriate behaviour and respect for others.
3. Understand the relationships between teachers and other professionals in education and training	3.1	Explain how the teaching role involves working with other professionals.
	3.2	Explain the boundaries between the teaching role and other professional roles.
	3.3	Describe points of referral to meet the individual needs of learners.

A TEACHER'S ROLE AND RESPONSIBILITIES IN EDUCATION AND TRAINING

1. Understand the teaching role and responsibilities in education and training.

The purpose of the unit is to enable the learner to understand the role and responsibilities of a teacher in lifelong learning and the relationship between different professionals in lifelong learning. It includes responsibility for maintaining a safe and supportive learning environment for learners.

Level 3 Assignment (Question Tips)

1.1 Explain the teaching role and responsibilities in education and training.

The teacher's role and responsibilities, for example:

- acting professionally and with integrity

- attending meetings and standardisation activities

- carrying out relevant administrative requirements

- communicating appropriately and effectively with learners and others

- completing attendance records/registers

- maintaining a safe, positive, and accessible learning environment for learners and others

- maintaining records and confidentiality

- partaking in quality assurance processes

- support learners and ensure learning is taking place.

- teaching and training in an inclusive, engaging, and motivating way

<u>Specific Roles</u>

- Support learners in all facets of learning.

Generic Teaching Roles

- Communicate knowledge and experience.
- Assist learners to develop practical skills.
- Guiding and mentoring learners to achieve their individual learning goals.

Generic Teaching Responsibilities

- Teachers have a duty to ensure the health and safety of their learners.
- Teachers are responsible for the moral and physical well-being of their learners when they are within the confines of the educational institution.
- They must stick to and maintain high professional standards.
- They must maintain technical competence in their area of expertise.

TASK 1

Roles
List your Teaching Roles

Responsibilities:

List Your responsibilities as a teacher.

Reference

Gravells (2014) Award in Education and Training (AET) pages 1-7

THE TEACHING CYCLE

This is a systematic process that every teacher or trainer goes through to ensure their learners' needs are met.

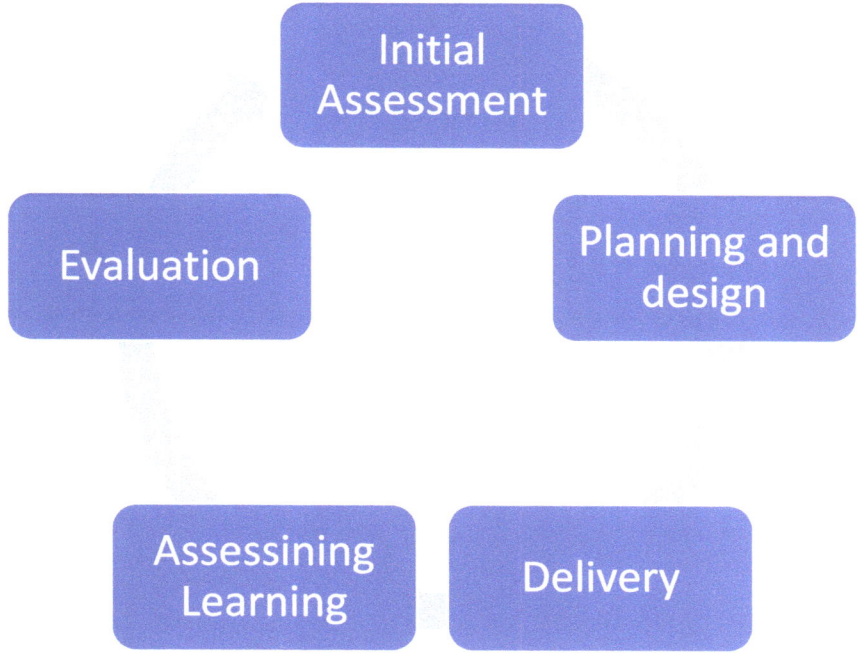

Initial Assessment

This involves finding out what the learners need, and you can find this out by sending the initial assessment form. The form includes information about why they are taking the course and what they hope to gain from the course.

INITIAL ASSESSMENT FORM **Key Task 2**

Title	

Name	

Date of Birth	

Address (with Post Code)	
Course Title	

Telephone number		Mobile Phone	

Delivery Method Required please Tick the box.

Blended learning ◯   Classroom ◯

Course Start date:

Course end Date:

Individual Declaration:

I confirm the accuracy of the information provided in this application form and wish to apply for the above-mentioned course in my name.

Signed

Academic Qualifications

Name of College /School	Date left	Subject studied	Grade

Vocational Qualifications

Name of college /work /establishment	Vocational Subject	Grade Gained and Year

---

Section 1: Background Knowledge

This section is about your roles, responsibilities, learning styles, the teaching cycle, section plan and selecting Resources.

Have you any previous experience with regard to the contents of this section?

Yes ☐   No ☐   Little Knowledge ☐

Level 3 Education and Training — Key Task 2

Section 2: Planning and Preparation Techniques

This section is about demonstrating planning and preparation and developing and adapting a session plan to meet the learner's needs.

Have you any experience with regards to the content of this section?

Yes ☐   No ☐   A little ☐

Section 3: Microteaching Session

The section is about teaching an inclusive microteaching section.

Have you any experience with regards to the contents of the session?

Yes ☐   No ☐   A little ☐

Section 4: Reflective Practice

This section is about providing motivational feedback and reflecting on delivery.

Have you any previous experience with regard to the content of this section?

Yes ☐   No ☐   A little ☐

If you have answered 'yes' or 'a little' with regards to any of the above, could you please describe in the space provided below your experience with regards to the relevant section?

Describe your experiences with regard to the sections provided above

LEVEL 3 EDUCATION AND TRAINING   KEY TASK 2

Please write what you think a prospective training provider or educational institution about the individual from this application form.

LEVEL 3 EDUCATION AND TRAINING   KEY TASK 2

> **Write what you think a prospective training provider or educational institution would not learn about the individual from this application form.**

PLANNING AND DESIGN

This involves you preparing your lesson plan and the resources you need for the delivery of the course to achieve the aims and learning outcomes of the course.

Planning and designing the course involves you establishing the aims and learning outcomes of the course. Through planning you can devise a session plan that meets the needs of the learners.

Establish the aims and learning outcomes of the course.

AIMS

This is a statement of what you intend to achieve.

Learning Outcomes

These are measurable outcomes that the learner will be able to know upon completion of the course. These are aims in small chunks which are normally expressed as assessment criteria that the learner is expected to achieve upon completion of the course.

A course without aims and learning outcomes will be said to be properly planned.

Group size, size of the classroom, duration of the course, and the learning environment.

Sufficient chairs and tables for learners. Can all learners see you from their seating position, do you have enough sockets for the equipment in the learning environment? Do you have enough refreshments for the delegates?

Seating Plan and Classroom arrangement

Theatre-style seating arrangement

Traditional /Examination seating arrangement

U- Shape seating arrangement

Chevron seating arrangement

Open circle seating arrangement

Boardroom seating arrangement

Closed circle seating arrangement.

FACILITATING LEARNING

This involves training, teaching, receiving and giving feedback, and carrying learning through the use of different learning resources.

ASSESSING LEARNING

You do this by checking if your learners have gained any knowledge or skill during your teaching. You can achieve this also by using formal and informal methods of assessment, and allowing your leaners to provide feedback on your teaching so you can improve your teaching skills.

EVALUATING LEARNING

Feedback from others, by evaluating every stage of the learning process to ensure your improvement.

Make sure the course/ learning is evaluated from beginning to finish.

A course evaluation should cover the following:

- The performance of the teacher/tutor
- Assessment methods
- Administration prior to, during, and at the end of the course.
- The training venue
- Methods employed during the delivery of the course.
- Were the needs of learners met?

The evaluation ideally should be recorded for training providers to monitor and for awarding organisations to confirm if their requirements are being met.

Recorded evaluations are also useful for standardisation purposes as the outcome of the evaluation can lead to improvements within the organisation.

DELIVERING THE COURSE

USE OF ICEBREAKERS

An icebreaker is a short task or activity introduced at the beginning of a session and intended to help members of a group begin the process of working together, create a positive working environment, or breakdown social barriers. They assist learners have an insight into each other.

Icebreakers are generally good, but they may also have some negative aspects. Be mindful of learners who are shy or nervous about expressing themselves in public. Typical reasons for this are- the learners may never have spoken in public before, they may be shy or they had a bad previous learning experience to ease the process, it is always good practice to engage the learners preferably on a one-to-one basis before the ice-breaking activity is introduced.

ENERGISERS

Usually introduced in the session when it appears that the learners are becoming tired. It is a useful motivating tool. They are most effectively employed after lunch when delegates are full and feel relaxed.

GROUP WORK

Creating group work can help create inclusion. It is better to select members of the group rather than allowing the group to select their members. By so doing, you can create a group where learners are able to learn from each other.

PERSONALITIES WITHIN THE GROUP

Look out for natural leaders within the group and monitor the effects they are having within the group. If it is a positive effect then encourage them but if their personality is affecting any or other members within the group, then intervene by removing or rotating the leadership. Also, look out for other members of the group who may be confident and find ways of including them in the group activities. The behavioural types within a group can be classified into- assertive, passive, or aggressive.

Assertive personalities- they make their needs known.

Passive personalities- will not make their needs openly known.

Aggressive- they will share their needs openly and sometimes in an intimidating manner.

LEGISLATION, REGULATORY REQUIREMENTS, AND CODES OF PRACTICE

Legislation, regulatory requirements, and codes of practice, for example:

The Data Protection Act 2018

According to this law, everyone responsible for using data should follow the "data protection principles." Teachers hold information about learners; therefore, you must comply with this law.

Health and Safety at Work etc Act (1974)

Your primary responsibility as a teacher is to ensure the health, safety, and well-being of your learners. To accomplish this, you should carry out a risk assessment of the classroom. Avoid trailing or damaged wires, sockets, and where there is sufficient heating and lighting within the training environment.

Human Rights Act 1998

This law safeguards the fundamental rights and freedoms of individuals. You must therefore protect the rights of learners to freedom of expression and diversity.

The Freedom of Information Act 2000

Under this law, public authorities are obligated to publish some of their activities and members of the public can request information from organisations.

Equality and Diversity, for example: The Equality Act (2010)

The Equality and Diversity Act ensures that everyone is protected from discrimination within the workplace. You should therefore ensure you are complying with this law by encouraging and promoting inclusion of all learners no matter their racial, ethnic, or sexual orientation.

Copyright Designs and Patents Act (1988)

Safeguarding Vulnerable Groups Act (2006)

Control of Substances Hazardous to Health (COSHH) Regulations (2002) for subjects which include the use of chemicals and hazardous materials.

Food Hygiene Regulations (2006) for subjects which include the use of food Health and Safety

(Display Screen Equipment) Regulations (1992) for subjects which include the use of computer screen.

Manual Handling Operation Regulations (1992) for subjects which include the lifting and carrying of items.

Codes of practice such as: Acceptable use of information technology, Timekeeping, Dress, etc.

REGULATORY REQUIREMENTS

OFQUAL, SQA ACCREDITATION AND QUALIFICATIONS WALES

Awarding bodies must run their courses in compliance with the requirements of these bodies and teachers who work for training providers must make sure they follow rules set by those awarding bodies.

CODES OF PRACTICE

These set out the parameters within which teachers must operate- how they should conduct themselves.

2014 Professional Standards:

These standards were issued by the Education and Training Foundation

Show commitment to the following in your professional practice.

Professional Values and Attributes

Develop your own judgment of what works and does not work in your teaching and training.

Professional Knowledge and Understanding

Develop deep and critically informed knowledge and understanding in theory and practice.

Professional Skills

Develop your expertise and skills to ensure the best outcomes for learners.

KEY TASK 3

1.2 Summarise key aspects of legislation, regulatory requirements, and codes of practice relating to your own role and responsibilities.

WAYS TO PROMOTE EQUALITY AND DIVERSITY

EQUALITY

It is a state of being equal. It also means fairness, and equality of opportunities. No one is treated unfavourably due to special characteristics.

The protection of different groups from discrimination and unfair treatment is enshrined in the Equality Act 2010.

Teachers must avoid any form of discrimination against the learner.

The special characteristics on the basis of which people discriminate are:

AGE

Disability

Gender Reassignment

Marriage and civil partnership

Pregnancy

Race

Religion or belief

Sex

Sexual orientation

Teachers must endeavour to promote equality within the learning environment, and they can do this in several ways such as:

Complying with the training provider's equality policy

Promoting anti-discrimination practices.

DIVERSITY

This is the practice or quality of including or involving people from different social and ethnic backgrounds and different genders, sexual orientations, etc. It is important that diversity needs to be considered when a course is being planned and designed.

Teachers must include anti-discriminatory practices when drawing up the ground rules for the course. Teachers need to make clear that no anti-discriminatory practices will be condoned in the learning environment.

TASK 4

1.3 Explain ways to promote equality and value diversity.

IDENTIFYING AND MEETING INDIVIDUAL LEARNER NEEDS

MASLOW'S HIERARCHY OF NEEDS

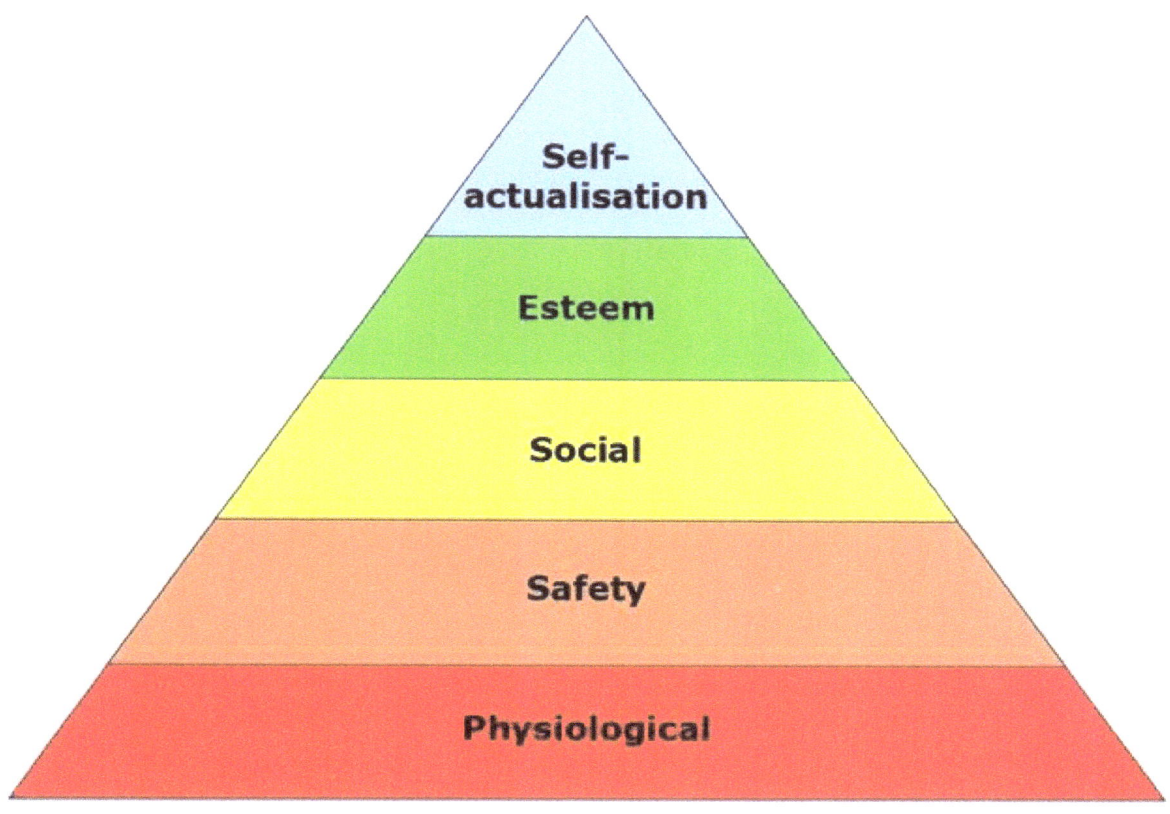

Maslow rejected the notion that the future of any human being is determined by what happened in their childhood. That everyone can achieve their goals if all obstacles are removed. He argued that there are 5 human needs that must be met.

The highest level is being self-actualisation-this the complete realisation of one's potential. Only a few people get to this level. Education, according to Maslow is the key to achieving this level. The other levels are self-esteem, recognition, safety/security, and psychological.

Self-actualisation- in relation to learning involves whether the learner is achieving their learning goals.

Self-esteem- is the learner learning something useful?

Recognition- Does the learner feel they belong and do they get the respect from others?

Safety/Security- does the learner feel safe within the learning environment/ are they happy or worried about anything?

Psychological- does the learner feel like the learning environment is comfortable? Are they hungry, thirsty, tired, or cold?

Learners' movement from one level to another depends on whether they have satisfied their needs at each level. Their progression from one level to the other depends on whether they are satisfied with the previous level.

The teacher's role is to make sure learners feel safe in their learning environment and that can help motivate them to want to progress their learning to a higher level.

HOW THE MARLOW'S HIERARCHY OF NEEDS APPLY TO THE CLASSROOM ENVIRONMENT

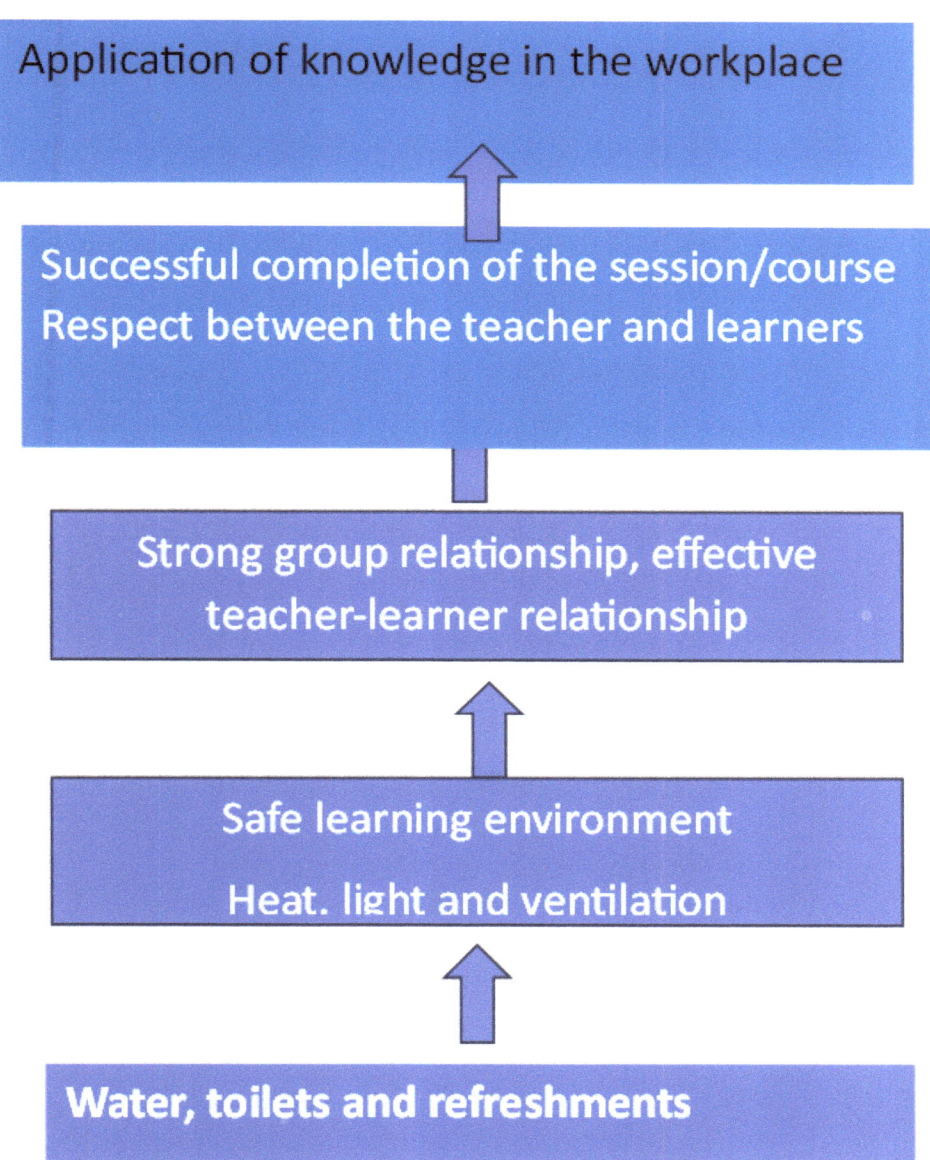

1.4 Explain why it is important to identify and meet individual learner needs.

Guide

Identifying and meeting individual learner needs, for example:

o identifying needs: information, advice, and guidance (IAG) interview, communicating with the learner prior to commencement, as part of the initial assessment process, during discussions at the interview stage, tutorial reviews

o needs: dyslexia, English as a second or other language, financial issues, health concerns, transport problems, etc.

o meeting needs: to improve motivation, attendance, progress, and achievement by providing additional support, and/or referring learners to appropriate people or agencies

Reasons why the learner completing the course and what they want to achieve from the course will assist you in building the session.

Are you meeting the learning styles of the learner? To achieve this, you have to adopt different methods such as visual, auditory, and kinaesthetic methods.

Make sure your knowledge of the subject you teach is up to date.

INDIVIDUAL LEARNER NEEDS

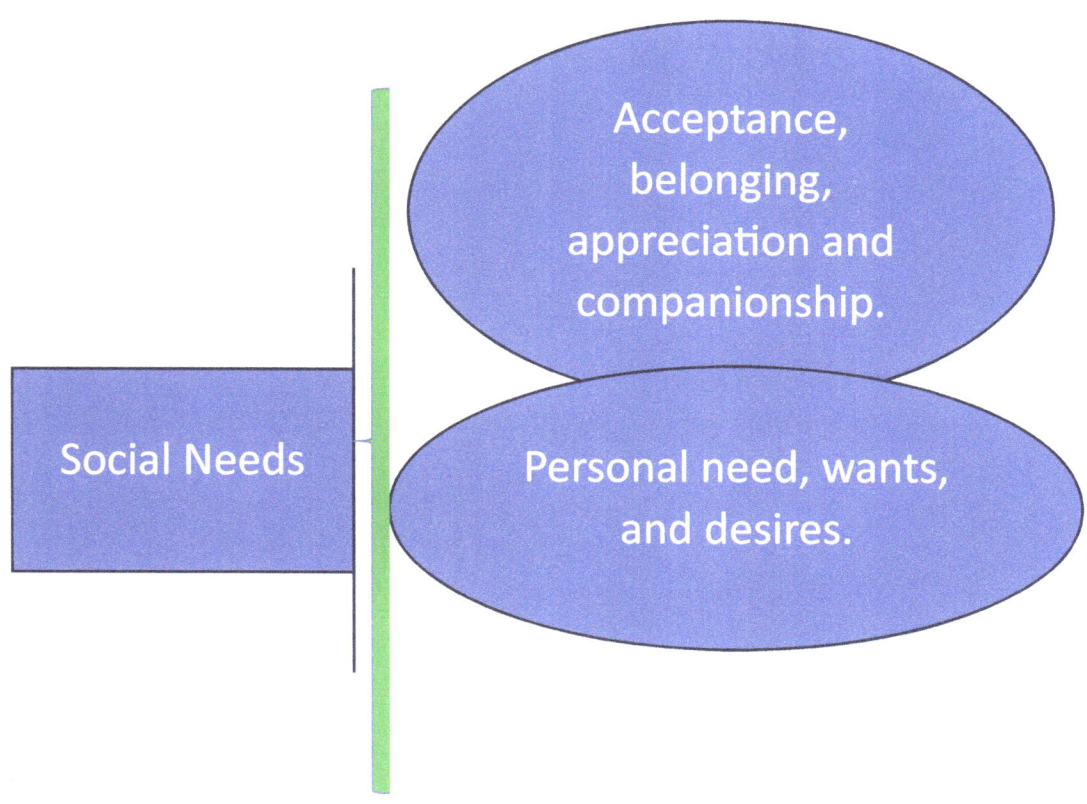

MEETING A LEARNERS LEARNING NEEDS

Initial assessment

Motivational factors

Meeting learning styles

Subject knowledge

Session planning

UNDERSTAND WAYS TO MAINTAIN A SAFE AND SUPPORTIVE LEARNING ENVIRONMENT

2.1 Explain ways to maintain a safe and supportive learning environment.

Project Tips

Maintaining a safe and supportive learning environment, for example:

- ensuring the physical, social, and learning aspects are appropriate, accessible, and suitable.
- health and safety
- safeguarding
  - Set out ground rules and allow the learners to be involved in the process so that they take ownership of it.

MAINTAIN A SAFE LEARNING ENVIRONMENT

- Safe classroom- by carrying out a risk assessment.
- Challenge unacceptable behaviour.
- Have policies available such as health and safety, equal opportunities, and referral policies. Awareness and access to these policies are crucial.

MAINTAIN A SUPPORTIVE LEARNING ENVIRONMENT

- Adopt a positive attitude.
- Motivate the learners.
- Be inclusive in your learning practices.
- Verbal and non-verbal communication must be used effectively.
- Have sufficient resources.

- Acknowledge contributions made by learners.
- Your learning outcomes must be realistic and achievable.

WAYS TO MAINTAIN A SAFE AND SUPPORTIVE LEARNING ENVIRONMENT.

Set	Set ground rules
Make	Make sure classroom is safe
Challenge	Challenge bad behaviour
Have	Have policies available

HOW TO MAINTAIN A SAFE AND SUPPORTIVE LEARNING ENVIRONMENT

- Positive attitude
- Motivate the learners
- Put referral procedures in place

- Adopt inclusive and learning practices

- Use verbal and non-verbal communication
- Have sufficient resources

- Learners should be encouraged to own their learning

- Set smart objectives

GROUP LEARNING NEEDS

The needs that a group of learners have must be met for learning to take place.

PROMOTING APPROPRIATE BEHAVIOUR AND RESPECT FOR OTHERS.

It is important for teachers to create a positive learning environment. Learners learn from what they see teachers do. It is therefore important that teachers promote appropriate behaviour by being well-behaved themselves. They must comply with the professional standards for teachers and trainers in education and training created by the Education and Training Foundation. Teachers are expected to comply with guidelines and laws that regulate their profession.

Appropriate behaviour and respect for others can be promoted also in the following ways:

- Being honest, reliable, and trustworthy

- Challenging and managing inappropriate behaviour

- Communicating appropriately

- Encouraging politeness and consideration towards others

- Leading by example

- Liaising and working with others in a professional manner.

- Listening to others' points of view

- To create an appropriate atmosphere in which learning can effectively take place.

- valuing others' opinions

Teachers must create appropriate behaviour and respect for others by:

| Adhering to professional standards / Create grounds regarding appropriate behaviour and respect for others | Create positive learning environment | Be honest, reliable, and trustworthy |

RELATIONSHIPS BETWEEN TEACHERS AND OTHER PROFESSIONALS IN EDUCATION AND TRAINING

The teacher's role involves working with other professionals. The teacher must maintain and establish professional relationships, and this can be accomplished in the following ways:

Working with other professionals

- Administration staff

- Assessors

- Internal and external quality assurers

- Health and safety officers

- Learning support staff

- Managers

- Reprographics staff

- Support workers.

- Technicians

You work with these professionals by attending departmental meetings.

Attending standardisation meetings, offering, and receiving support and learning from subject experts on learning disabilities, dyslexia, dyspraxia

Meeting IQAs.

By interacting with other professionals, teachers can learn and share best practices from each other.

HOW A TEACHER CAN ESTABLISH AND MAINTAIN PROFESSIONAL RELATIONSHIPS

- Attend departmental meetings.
- Meeting internal quality assurance personnel
- Attend standardisation meeting.
- Meeting with the line manager
- Meeting internal quality assurance personnel
- Collaborate with agencies and other organisations.

BOUNDARIES BETWEEN THE TEACHING ROLE AND OTHER PROFESSIONAL ROLES.

Teachers have personal as well as professional boundaries within their teaching role for example,

- Knowing the boundaries of the teaching role i.e., knowing where the teaching role stops and not overstepping it.

- Not doing something which is part of someone else's role.

- Not blurring the teaching role with a supportive and/or assessment or another role

- Not putting the professional role under pressure from managers, targets, or funding

PERSONAL BOUNDARIES

Know the limits of your knowledge- if you do not know something then ask colleagues with a better grasp of the subject.

Only give advice that you have the authority to give.

Stick to regulatory requirements for example the professional standards for teachers and trainers in education and training.

Complying with assessment requirements of awarding organisations.

PROFESSIONAL BOUNDARIES

You are bound by professional codes of conduct, and departmental procedures. Very important to stick to the limitations of your authority.

BOUNDARIES BETWEEN THE TEACHING ROLE AND OTHER PROFESSIONAL ROLES

Boundaries-Personal

- Limit of your knowledge
- Acceptable advice
- Constraints imposed
- Adhering to regulatory requirements
- Assessment requirements

Boundaries-Professional

- Knowing the limit of your authority
- Adhering to professional codes of conduct
- Adhering to internal departmental procedure

POINTS OF REFERRAL TO MEET THE INDIVIDUAL NEEDS OF LEARNERS

These are reference points for learners to cater for their educational or physical needs.

Points of referral to meet individual needs:

- Local library or internet café, specialist colleagues and/or training programmes

- Relevant support agencies, telephone helplines, Citizens Advice Bureau

- Health centres, general practitioners, hospitals

- National Careers Service

- Specialist staff internal or external to the organisation

Other points of referral are:

External quality assurance

Awarding organisations

Departmental Heads

Funding specialists

Internal Quality Assurer

Support workers.

Managers

Other teachers

Colleges

POINTS OF REFERRAL — KEY TASKS 5

With reference to your teaching role, list the points of referral that are available and underneath each one, describe how they meet the needs of your learners.

1.

2.

3.

4.

5.

6.

7.

REFLECTION ON UNIT 1

What have I learnt or found to be beneficial after completing this unit?

What action do I now take to improve my knowledge and directly benefit my learners?

UNDERSTANDING AND USING INCLUSIVE TEACHING AND LEARNING APPROACHES IN EDUCATION AND TRAINING

1.1 Describe features of inclusive teaching and learning.

Features of inclusive teaching and learning, for example:

- ascertaining individual needs, learning preferences and goals

- challenging stereotyping, discrimination, and prejudice as it occurs.

- differentiating activities to address individual differences; for example, different abilities and levels

- ensuring the environment is accessible to all learners.

- identifying where modifications or changes are needed to equipment or activities.

- recognising and valuing individual learner contributions and achievements

- using a wide range of teaching, learning, and assessment approaches based upon learner needs.

- using resources and materials which positively promote all aspects of community and society, equality, and diversity.

Compare the strengths and limitations of teaching and learning approaches used in your own area of specialism in relation to meeting individual learners needs.

Teaching and Learning approach	Strength	Limitation
Group work	Learners learn from their peers	Shy and quiet learners may find this uncomfortable.
Questions and Answers	This provides a quick formative assessment	There may not be sufficient time to reach all learners in a large group.
Icebreakers	Icebreakers help to introduce learners and establish a rapport between learners and teacher	Shy or quiet learners may find this embarrassing.
Group feedback	The group may learn from the feedback provided	Individuals in the group may prefer to receive their feedback individually.

PROVIDING DEVELOPMENT OPPORTUNITIES [ENGLISH, MATHEMATICS, AND ICT]

Opportunities for English, maths, ICT, and wider skills enable learners to function confidently, effectively, and independently in their personal and professional lives.

English: Reading, writing, listening, speaking, discussing Maths: approximations, estimations, calculations, measurements allow learners to practise the spoken English and perfect their interpersonal skills. When learners are given assignments they encourage learners to improve their written English and when they use PowerPoint during their delivery of they can practise their reading skills.

ICT: Allowing learners to produce their assignments on computer builds their ICT skills and enables them to improve their written skills as well. When learners carry out their research on the internet and on computer they improve their computer skills and they also improve their knowledge of available technology such e-learning, PowerPoint, video, and DVD.

Using smart phones, computers, tablets, laptops etc for e-mail, web-based research, social networking, watching videos, using presentation packages, word processors, spreadsheets, databases for projects, virtual learning environments (VLE) for accessing and submitting resources, materials, and assignments help to improve the ICT skills of the learners.

Mathematics: When teachers incorporate adding, subtracting, multiplications and percentages to assignments, they encourage learners to improve their mathematics skills.

Wider skills: Group work and activities to promote: Citizenship, Employability, Enterprise, Social Responsibility, Sustainability, Working with Others, Problem Solving, Improving own Learning and Performance.

PLANNING AN INCLUSIVE TEACHING AND LEARNING

This part of the course is aimed at ensuring you understand the use of inclusive teaching and learning approaches to meet the needs of the learners.

The learning approaches are the methods that you will use to deliver your teaching. As a teacher, this will involve your style of delivery, the resources that you use, your assessment method or whether group work is used. All these approaches must be inclusive to ensure the learners are motivated and engaged.

2. Understand ways to create an inclusive teaching and learning environment

According to Maslow's hierarchy of needs, there are six levels of needs. The first level is the physiological needs which include the basic and essential needs of life such as(Gorman 2010)[1]food water and shelter. The basic needs of students need to be met before the second level of needs can be satisfied. The second level is safety.

All students need to feel safe in their learning environment. A student needs to know that they will not be harmed in the environment in which they are studying. The first and second levels of needs must be satisfied before the student's third level of needs can be met. The third level relates to a student having a feeling of belongingness and love. Students want to feel that they are part of a group or group of students. They cannot really learn in an environment where they do not feel like they fit in. At the fourth level, students ought to have satisfied the first,

---

[1] Gorman, D. (2010). Maslow's hierarchy and social and emotional wellbeing. *Aboriginal & Islander Health Worker Journal*, *34* (1), 27-29.

second, and third hierarchy of needs before reaching the fourth level of needs. The fourth level requires the students to meet esteem needs. The role of the teacher at this level is to make sure that the self-esteem of students needs to be enhanced through recognition of hard work and achievements.

To attain the final level of needs which is self-actualisation, students ought to have satisfied the four previous levels of needs. The fifth level is the self-actualisation-where students find ways to realise their potential for learning. At this level, students set their learning goals and seek to realise them. The goals might be that they want to achieve the best grade on a course or achieve the best result in their course. The sixth level is attained when learners have achieved all the goals of the other levels and are now concerned with what is called self-transcendence. (Gorman, 2010) at this level, students are not really concerned with their own personal goals but how to help other students achieve their own goals. By helping other students, they can have a better learning experience.

The teacher's role in the classroom is to make sure that students meet all the different levels of Maslow's learning hierarchy to foster their motivation to learn. McLeod, 2007 said when students have met all the levels of Maslow's hierarchy of needs, the students are at their full potential of learning. A student who has achieved all the levels of the hierarchy is more likely to be better motivated and will be better than most students who have not attained that level.[2]

Learners with disabilities or special needs find it difficult to be motivated to learn and therefore require teachers who will motivate them by fostering a sense of belonging. Teachers must understand why certain learners are having trouble learning if they happen to fall under the category of learners who are struggling with meeting their basic needs. A poor student may not learn at the same level as

---

[2] McLeod, S. A. (2007). *Maslow's Hierarchy of Needs.* Retrieved from http://www.simplypsychology.org/maslow.html

their rich counterpart because the basic needs of the rich student are met, and the poor student is therefore disadvantaged by the socio-economic deprivations. It is therefore important that a teacher does not categorise the student with the poor background as an underachiever and seek to find ways to help the poor child to overcome the difficulties responsible for their poor achievement.

"Carl Rogers believed that humans have one basic motive that is the tendency to self-actualize - i.e., to fulfill one's potential and achieve the highest level of 'human-beingness' we can. Like a flower that will grow to its full potential if the conditions are right, but which is constrained by its environment, so people will flourish and reach their potential if their environment is good enough."[3]

2.1 Explain why it is important to create an inclusive teaching and learning environment.

An inclusive learning environment is one where all learners are included in

all activities and where they feel valued by their teachers and peers. An inclusive learning environment helps to strengthen the learning process.

Furthermore, it motivates learners to want to succeed. A non-inclusive environment can be a demotivating factor which can result in absenteeism.

Features of inclusive teaching and learning, for example:

- Ascertaining individual needs, learning preferences, and goals

- Challenging stereotyping, discrimination, and prejudice as it occurs.

---

[3] Carl Rogers McLeod, S. A. (2007). Carl Rogers. Retrieved from http://www.simplypsychology.org/carl-rogers.html.

- Differentiating activities to address individual differences, for example, different abilities and levels.

- Ensuring the environment is accessible to all learners.

- Identifying where modifications or changes are needed to equipment or activities.

- Recognising and valuing individual learner contributions and achievements

- Using a wide range of teaching, learning, and assessment approaches based upon learner needs.

- Using resources and materials which positively promote all aspects of community and society, equality, and diversity.

TEACHING AND LEARNING APPROACH

2.2 Explain why it is important to select teaching and learning approaches, resources, and assessment methods to meet individual learner needs.

TEACHING AND LEARNING APPROACHES.

It is vital to select teaching and learning approaches that are engaging and serve to motivate learners.

The following are examples of learning and teaching approaches:

Collaborative learning: where two or more people learn something together, share their experiences and resources.

Discussion groups: ideas from different perspectives are discussed by the Group.

Group work: Learners learn from their peers and find common solutions to problems.

Projects: learners work together with peer groups to plan, and design something as a group or individually.

Assignment: This involves research carried out by learners to find solutions to questions asked.

SELECTING TEACHING AND LEARNING RESOURCES

There are three main teaching resources:

Facilities

People - The teachers must work with other professionals for the benefit of learners and themselves. If a learner is faced with learning challenges, you should be able to refer them to another professional with the skill to deal with the issue. The people you may want to refer to are referral specialists, other teachers, experts in certain subject matter, internal quality assurers, and funding specialists.

Material and equipment - These are resources that the teacher usually uses during their lessons /sessions. Examples are handouts, evaluation form. In terms of the materials the following guidelines must be followed:

The supporting materials must be visible, good quality, the materials must be clear and straight to the point. They must be accurate and must support the topic being delivered.

SELECTING TEACHING AND LEARNING ASSESSMENT METHODS

It is difficult to match assessment methods with each individual learning needs. Assessment methods are normally prescribed by the awarding organisation if the courses being delivered lead to formal assessment.

Visual learners often prefer written assessments that have pictures and written instructions.

Auditory learners often prefer the verbal question-and-answer method of assessment. They also like group activities and discussions.

Kinaesthetic learners: Prefer practical assessment. They like trying their hands on new practical skills.

The formative assessments used by teachers are those based on the individual or group needs. Examples of these types of formative assessment are: MCQs (multiple-choice questions, written assessments, quizzes, verbal questions, and answer sessions, practical assessments, and self-assessment.

Guide

Strengths and limitations of teaching and learning approaches, for example, those applicable to:

- Demonstrations
- Discussions
- Distance, open, or e-learning.
- Group work.
- Instruction

- Practical activities
- Presentations
- Questions and answers
- Research
- Role plays.
- Seminars
- Technology-based teaching and learning.

ENGAGING AND MOTIVATING LEARNERS

2.3   Explain ways to engage and motivate learners.

INTRINSIC MOTIVATION

This is an internal desire to complete a task or goal.

EXTRINSIC MOTIVATION

This comes from external rewards. This is usually provided by the teacher. The motivation in this case comes from the teacher's praise or reward of the learner. This can be triggered by feedback from both the learner and the teachers.

There are different methods of engaging and motivating learners. All these methods will assist in the learning process and aid in meeting individual and group learning needs.

Engaging and motivating learners, for example, by:

- Asking open questions
- Being aware of attention-span time limits
- Giving ongoing constructive, supportive, and developmental feedback
- Giving praise and encouragement
- Setting realistic aims and objectives
- Stretching learners' potential
- Supporting those who need it.
- Treating learners with respect and as individuals

- Using activities to get learners actively working together.

- Varying teaching, learning, and assessment approaches to reach all learning preferences.

GROUND RULES

2.4 Summarise ways to establish ground rules with learners.

These are boundaries set or rules agreed upon between teachers and learners for the overall benefit of every member of the group.

Ground rules can be established verbally, visually on PowerPoint, on a flip chart or handout and it can also be sent to delegates prior to the commencement of the course as part of a pre-course package. It is important the ground rules are set at the beginning of the course so that everyone is aware of the standard or what is expected of them from the start of the course. Examples of ground rules are switching off electronic devices, arriving on time, respecting others, how to indicate when you want to ask questions, smoking must take place outside the building in nominated areas, where to assemble in the event of a fire outbreak.

Establishing ground rules, for example, by:

- Activities, discussions, group work, icebreakers, role plays, etc.

- Deciding and agreeing on what is negotiable and non-negotiable.

PLANNING AN INCLUSIVE TEACHING AND LEARNING

This part of the course is aimed at ensuring you understand the use of inclusive teaching and learning approaches to meet the needs of the learners.

The learning approaches are the methods that you will use to deliver your teaching. As a teacher, this will involve your style of delivery, the resources that you use, your assessment method or whether group work is used. All these approaches must be inclusive to ensure the learners are motivated and engaged.

LEARNING STYLES

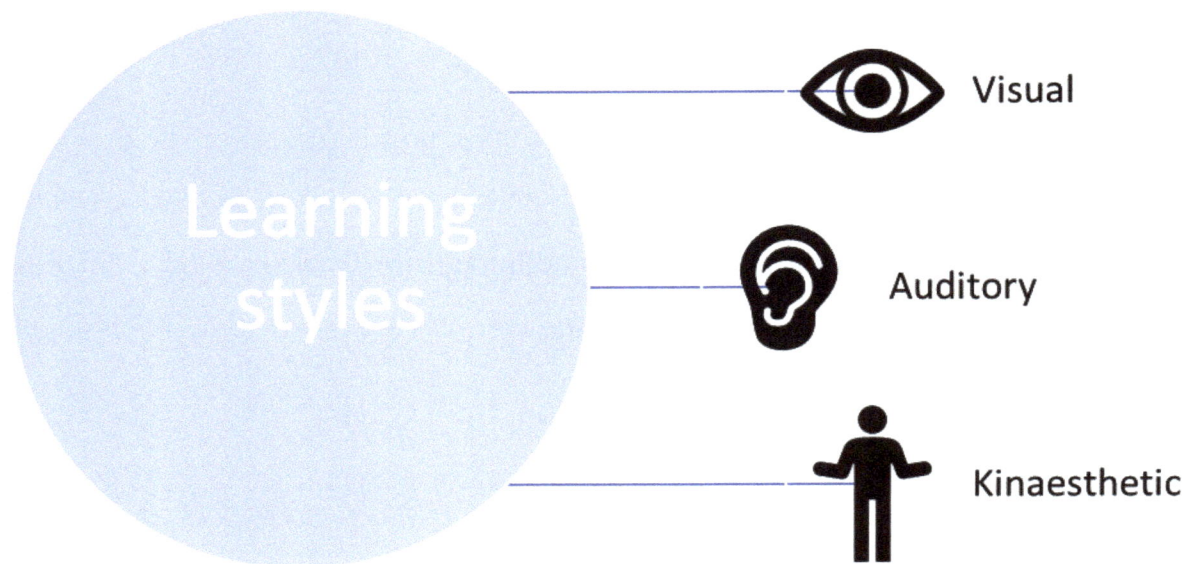

4. Be able to deliver inclusive teaching and learning

Learning styles
Visual

Visual learners are good at completing tasks once they have read the instructions. Reading books, looking at pictures, diagrams, handouts, and watching videos

Auditory

These learners learn by listening and will remember lyrics to songs.

Kinaesthetic learning

Learning through carrying out physical activity- touching, feeling, and doing.

This category of learners tends to try things out rather than following instructions.

Types of visual aids used in presentation:

75 of what we know comes to us visually.

- PowerPoint.
- Whiteboards.
- Video clips.
- Charts and graphs.
- Handouts.
- Flip chart.
- Props.
- Overheads.

WHAT IS LEARNING?

Learning is the acquisition knowledge and skills through being taught something new and being able to demonstrate it.

Learning can be either formal or informal

Formal Learning:

This is structured through lectures, case studies and books

Informal Learning

Experience and through our subconscious

Formal learning is **familiar and straightforward**

Experiential learning, learning through experience is haphazard and messy.

KOLB'S EXPERIENTIAL LEARNING THEORY/LEARNING STYLE MODEL

Kolb was of the view that our experiences have an impact on the learning process. Experiential learning is a four-stage process:

CONCRETE EXPERIENCE- where the learner has a new experience or interprets an old experience in a new way. For example, a first-aid student learns practical CPR for the first time.

REFLECTIVE OBSERVATION

This is when the learner reflects on a new experience to have a better understanding of what it is. The first-time CPR learner reflects on their first practice and suggests what they could have done to make their first attempt better.

ABSTRACT CONCEPTUALISATION

This is when the learner adapts their thinking or constructs new ideas based on their new experience.

Classroom will create or would have created a better learning experience.

ACTIVE EXPERIMENTATION

The learner tries out what they have learnt.

KOLB'S LEARNING STYLES

KOLBS LEARNING STYLES

- **CONCRETE EXPERIENCE-** UNDERGOING THE EXPEREINCE
- **REFLECTIVE OBSERVATION-** Thinking about the experience
- **ABSTRACT CONCEPTUALISATION-** rflecting on the process and how it could be improved
- **ACTIVE EXPERIEMENTATION-** starting the routine again and implementing any changes

Exercise:

Give examples of how you learn from experience.

LEARNING STYLES

Honey and Mumford styles of learning

- **Activists**
- **Pragmatists**
- **Theorists**
- **Reflectors**

ACTIVISTS: -

- These learners learn by doing and doing something immediately.
- They wait and listen to all the instructions, to read the manual first but to get on with the job.
- They will try and find out if it works.
- When asked questions, they will answer immediately without waiting to work it out fully.

- They tend to be enthusiastic about new things and like lots of new experiences. They want to try anything once! When they finish one activity, they want to pass onto the next one.
- They want to see as many new things as possible.
- They will often volunteer to lead an activity.

Activities to try out with activists.

- Role play
- Competitions
- Problem solving
- Puzzles
- Group discussions.

Pragmatists

- These learners like to experiment, to apply new insights.
- When these learners have received new training, they will be full of enthusiasm and full of new ideas they will want to try out.

- These learners do not go by what they have been told until they have seen it with their own eyes. "It may work for you, but I want to see it work for me."
- They try to find new and more effective ways of doing things.
- They take shortcuts or devise new modes of working.
- They tend to be confident, energetic, and impatient about what they see as too much talk.
- They are problem solvers and see new situations as a challenge from which they can learn.
- They like to be shown how to do something but become frustrated if they are not allowed to do it for themselves.
- They do not like to learn a subject if it does not mean anything to them.

Activities to try out with pragmatists.

- Case studies
- Problem solving
- Discussions
- Think about how to apply the learning in reality… "what's in it for me?"

THEORISTS

- These learners like to build systems, to get down to just principles.
- They do not want to deal with real case they are thought to be too limiting, rather than understand the whole, general principle first.
- Learners speak in general rather than in concrete terms.
- They will always question basic assumptions.
- They make rules out of cases.

- They will always think problems through step by step.
- They try to make coherent pictures out of complete material.
- They often represent ideas in diagrams showing relationships.
- They try to be objective, detailed, they are less sympathetic to human feelings, to other people's subjective judgments.
- These people want the world to be logical.

Activities to try out with

THEORISTS

- Applying theories
- Background information
- Statistics
- Quotes
- Models

REFLECTORS

- These learners best learn by observing and thinking about what has happened, so like to wait and see. They will watch others conducting a task and listen to talk of others.
- These learners do not give the first answer that comes to their head, when they are asked a question, they take their time, think about it and they hesitate and are often uncertain..
- They want more information before when they give a true answer.
- These learners tend to like to share their learning with others because these helps to collect different opinions before they make when they up their own minds.

Activities to try out with reflectors.

- Paired discussions
- Observing others
- Feedback from others
- Coaching
- Self-analyses work
- Time out to observe.

4.1 Use teaching and learning approaches, resources, and assessment methods to meet individual learner needs.

Resources, for example:

- Handouts, working models, interactive whiteboards, ICT, flipcharts, videos, textbooks, people i.e., visiting speaker, etc.

- How they can meet individual learner needs Assessment approaches, for example:

  - Assignments
  - Case studies
  - Observations
  - Puzzles and quizzes
  - Questions: oral and written.
  - Tests and exams

Please circle the one response from each question that best describes your most likely action.

1. If buying a present for yourself, what will you choose?
   a. A book
   b. A CD
   c. Tools or Gadgets

2. If given a piece of equipment to operate, what would you do?
   a. Read the instructions fully first.
   b. Listen to an experienced operator give an explanation.
   c. Have a go and learn through trial and error.

3. Which of the following would you most likely say in conversation?
   a. I see what you mean.
   b. I hear what you are saying.
   c. I know how you feel.

4. If teaching a person to do a practical task how would you prefer to do it?
   a. Give them written instructions.
   b. Show them how to do it.
   c. Tell me how to do it.

5. How would you drive a new car?
   a. Read the instructions fully first.
   b. Listen to an experienced operator give an explanation.
   c. Have a go and learn through trial and error.

6. If your friend showed you their latest electronic device, which of the following would most likely say?

   a. Show me how it works.

   b. Tell me how it works.

   c. Let me have a go with it.

7. You have taken a wrong turn and got lost. What would you do?

   a. Look at a map.

   b. Ask for directions.

   c. Try to find the route yourself.

8. You decide to cook something different and new. How do you do it?

   a. Follow a recipe.

   b. Call a friend for an explanation.

   c. Follow your instincts and taste as you cook.

9. You arrive home and find a purchase faulty. What would you do?

   a. Email the store to complain.

   b. Telephone the store to complain.

   c. Return the item immediately to the store.

10. How do you choose a holiday?

    a. Read the brochures.

    b. Listen to the recommendations.

    c. Imagine the experience

11. How do you prefer to spend any spare time you have?

    a. Visiting museums and galleries

b. Enjoy music and conversation.   c. Playing sports and carrying DIY.
12. You are buying a new piece of clothing for yourself. Do you?   a. Look at it and imagine what it would be like.   b. Discuss the garment with the staff.   c. Try it on and test how it fits.
13. Mostly A's you have a visual preference   Mostly B's you have an auditory preference.   Mostly C's you have a kinaesthetic preference.

GROUP C UNDERSTANDING ASSESSMENT IN EDUCATION AND TRAINING

Level 3

Credit Value: 3

Unit summary

The purpose of this unit is to enable the learner to understand how different types and methods of assessment are used in education and training. It includes ways to involve learners in assessment and requirements for record keeping.

Learning outcomes	Assessment criteria
The learner will:	The learner can:
1. Understanding types and methods of assessment used in education and training	1.1 Explain the purposes of types of assessment used in education and training. (see Gravells AET pages 55, 146, 153, 154) 1.2 Describe characteristics of different methods of assessment in education and training. 1.3 Compare the strengths and limitations of different assessment methods in relation to meeting individual learner needs. (Gravells AET pages 158-169

	1.4 Explain how different assessment methods can be adapted to meet individual learner needs. (see Gravells AET page 171)
2. Understanding how to invoke learners and others in the assessment process.	2.1 Explain why it is important to involve learners and others in the assessment process.) Gravells AET page 171 2.2 Explain the role and use of peer- and self-assessment in the assessment process. (Gravells AET pages 172-174) 2.3 Identify sources of information that should be made available to learners and others involved in the assessment process. (Gravells AET 171)
3. Understand the role and use of constructive feedback in the assessment process	3.1 Describe key features of constructive feedback. 3.2 Explain how constructive feedback contributes to the assessment process. (Gravells Pages 175 3.3 Explain ways to give constructive feedback to learners.
4. Understand requirements for keeping records of assessment in education and training	4.1 Explain the need to keep records of assessment of learning.

	4.2 Summarise the requirements for keeping records of assessment in an organisation. (Gravells pages 13-15

THE PURPOSES OF TYPES OF ASSESSMENT USED IN EDUCATION AND TRAINING

Types of assessment

- **Initial assessment**
- Diagnostic
- Formative
- Holistic
- Summative

INITIAL ASSESSMENT

This is a means of gathering information.

Purpose of the initial assessment

- It helps to plan the structure of the course.
- It helps to determine the pitch and pace of the session.

Forms of initial assessment

- By way of application form
- By telephone call
- By Interview
- Skills test
- By Psychometric test

FORMATIVE ASSESSMENT

This is a continuous method of assessment carried out all through the course.

You are constantly assessing the learners to confirm that they have understood what you have taught. This can be done by multiple-choice tests- good for large groups of learners but can also be time-consuming and difficult to write group exercises or oral questions. This can be time-consuming when you are dealing with a large group of learners.

SUMMATIVE ASSESSMENT

This is a final assessment that is carried out at the end of the course.

CHARACTERISTICS OF DIFFERENT METHODS OF ASSESSMENT IN EDUCATION AND TRAINING

Assessment methods are intended to meet the needs of the learners and the assessment criteria of the learning outcome.

Must be designed for the ability and level of the learner for example level 1, 2, 3, or 4.

Designed to meet formal or informal requirements. Formal requirements:- used to measure the achievement at the end of the course. Summative assessment e.g., recorded for audit trail purposes.

Informal requirements: - used to measure learners understanding and progress on the course.

Must meet the requirements of what is being delivered.

May be stipulated by an awarding organisation or certificating body.

Peer and self-assessment, for example:

- Peer assessment involves a learner assessing another learner's progress.

- Self-assessment involves a learner assessing their own progress.

- The advantages and disadvantages of both

- Encouraging learners to make decisions about what has been learnt so far, take responsibility for their learning and become involved with the assessment process.

COMPARE THE STRENGTHS AND LIMITATIONS OF DIFFERENT ASSESSMENT METHODS IN RELATION TO MEETING INDIVIDUAL LEARNER NEEDS

STRENGTHS AND LIMITATIONS OF DIFFERENT ASSESSMENT METHODS

ASSESSMENT METHOD	STRENGTH	LIMITATION
Initial Assessment Application form Telephone call	You can gather information easily	Someone else may complete the application form on behalf of the learner.
Formative Question and answer. MCQ (Multiple-choice Questions)	It is an easy way of assessing a group of learners. An easy way of assessing knowledge of different parts of the course	It is time-consuming. It takes time for a large group of delegates to carry out this assessment. Learners may guess answers- it is therefore not an accurate way of assessing knowledge
Summative Written assessment Practical assessment	Can assess knowledge from all aspects of the course. Confirms that a practical skill has been learnt.	The answer to the question depends on how the learner perceives the question. The learner does not learn kinaesthetically.

ADAPTING THE ASSESSMENT METHODS TO MEET THE NEEDS OF THE LEARNERS

The assessment methods may be adapted to meet the needs of the learners. The reason for this is because the learners are not engaged. The assessment method may need to be adapted to ensure that the learning styles of the learner are considered or if the answers obtained from the learner are wrong and if the chosen assessment method is taking too long.

If the assessment method has been designed by the awarding organisation, there will be some inflexibility in trying to adapt it. This is not often a major issue as awarding organisations have reasonable adjustments policy which can be resorted to if the learner requires additional needs. For example, if the learner has dyslexia, it means that they will need further assistance in their examination or assessment. This means the awarding organisation can vary their assessment to aid the learner.

Formative assessment designed by a teacher which goes on all through the course is more flexible. If there is a need to adapt the assessment, the session plan should equally be amended to reflect the changes.

EXPLAIN WHY IT IS IMPORTANT TO INVOLVE LEARNERS AND OTHERS IN THE ASSESSMENT PROCESS

The aims of involving learners in the assessment process are:

- To allow learners to take ownership of their learning.
- It allows learners to have a record of their achievements.
- It heightens understanding and instils motivation.
- To enable learners to record their own progress, teachers can design an ILP) Individual learning plan.
- Ensuring learners are fully briefed and agree to appropriate activities and target dates.
- Taking individual learner needs into account.
- Ascertaining and building on prior learning and experience
- Enabling the learner to discuss what progress they are making.
- Involving others who are associated with the learner, for example, other assessors, workplace supervisors, etc, to ensure they are aware of progress and achievement.

HOW TO INVOLVE LEARNERS AND OTHERS IN THE ASSESSMENT PROCESS

The learner should always be involved in the assessment process from the beginning of the assessment to the end.

By providing an initial assessment to the learner, their prior learning, current skills and knowledge are established. The initial assessment provided an effective means of planning the course. But whilst the initial assessment gives the learner an opportunity to state their concerns, they might not always be truthful about the information included in the initial assessment form.

At the end of the session, you can use a quiz to determine what they have learnt during the courses. Asking the learners how they feel they are progressing on the course is another way of involving the learners.

PEOPLE THAT MAY BE INVOLVED IN THE ASSESSMENT PROCESS

IQAs

Invigilators

Teachers

Quality assurance personnel

Awarding organisations

Managers

Supervisors

Why involve others in the assessment process?

To ensure the assessment is fit for purpose- valid, authentic, current, sufficient, and reliable (VACSR)

EXPLAIN THE ROLE AND USE OF PEER AND SELF-ASSESSMENT IN THE ASSESSMENT PROCESS

Peer and self-assessment

- Peer assessment involves a learner assessing another learner's progress.

- Self-assessment involves a learner assessing their own progress.

- The advantages and disadvantages of both

- Encouraging learners to make decisions about what has been learnt so far, take responsibility for their learning and become involved with the assessment process.

The role of self-assessment in the assessment process

- It promotes reflective practice.
- It identifies the learner's strengths and weaknesses.
- It measures knowledge and competencies.
- It measures competence against standards.
- It allows for planning.

What is the role of peer assessment?

- Peer assessment allows learners to learn from each other.
- It allows learners to compare their progress with other learners.
- Provide feedback.
- It leads to the sharing of ideas.
- Sharing strategies
- Promotes group work.

WHAT IS FEEDBACK?

'Information about a person's performance of a task, etc. which is used as a basis for improvement.'

Types of Feedback

- Constructive feedback- motivates the learner.
- Destructive feedback- demotivates the learner.

Features of constructive feedback

Offer encouragement.

- Refer only to the aspects of performance that can be changed. It is futile and unhelpful to offer feedback on aspects of the learner's performance that cannot be altered through feedback.

- Be descriptive and the learner is clear about what you are saying.

- Stand by your feedback even when the learner disagrees with it.

- Offer factual feedback on what has occurred

- Give timely feedback. The feedback must be close to the event for which you are providing feedback.

- End on a positive note- praise the learner.

Giving feedback

Hot feedback must be given contemporaneously immediately after the event.

Give on a one-t-one basis or the group.

It should be motivational and encouraging.

The feedback should be given in parts.

First Part- start off with a praise "excellent work." Then deal with what went well. The parts that didn't go well should be presented in a way that is motivational.

Finish off the feedback with what went well and encourage the learner. Give the learner the chance to comment on their work too.

RECEIVING FEEDBACK

When receiving feedback, make sure you respond to the person giving the feedback, reflect on the feedback. You should encourage learners to give their own feedback on the learning session. This will lead to the further development of the course.

IDENTIFY SOURCES OF INFORMATION THAT SHOULD BE MADE AVAILABLE TO LEARNERS AND OTHERS INVOLVED IN THE ASSESSMENT PROCESS

These sources of information are required to enable learners to know what is required to claim competence in a subject or what is required to pass an assessment. The sources of information enable learners to know who to contact in the case of a complaint, or if they need to clarify issues regarding their qualification

Sources of information for learners and others, for example:

- The standards, qualification, job role, or units to be assessed.
- Assessment plans
- Feedback records
- Websites, textbooks, and journals
- Progress and achievement records

Evaluation forms

Tutor evaluation forms

Quality assurance documentation

Grievance policies and procedures

Data protection policy

Reasonable adjustments

Invigilation documentation

EXPLAIN THE NEED FOR KEEPING RECORDS OF ASSESSMENT OF LEARNING

An awarding organisation may require the records of the assessment to be kept or this may be in satisfaction of an audit trail, to create statistics or assist in learners' enquiries.

The need to keep records of assessment, for example:

- To show an audit trail of progress and achievement in case of an appeal for internal and external quality assurance purposes for funding purposes to comply with relevant legislation, policies, and procedures. This may be a requirement by Ofqual. Ofqual requires records of assessment to be kept for 3 years.

SUMMARISE THE REQUIREMENTS FOR KEEPING RECORDS OF ASSESSMENT IN AN ORGANISATION

The need to keep records of assessment, for example:

• To show an audit trail of progress and achievement in case of an appeal for internal and external quality assurance purposes for funding purposes to comply with relevant legislation, policies, and procedures.

Types-

Paper-based and data-based.

Record keeping is an important part of the role of a teacher.

What is the sort of records that are kept?

Paper-based or data-based. Both have secured safely.

Paper examinations

Audio or video recordings

Teaching logs

Signed appeals procedure.

Application forms

Funding documentation.

Why are records kept?

Records are often kept because it is the requirement of a college, Ofqual, or an awarding body. Records show evidence of standardisation and evidence that assessment criteria have been met and are also evidence of an audit trail. Records are also kept because it is a requirement of internal quality assurance process. When external quality assurance is sent by awarding bodies, they examine the records of training providers as part of the process.

Awarding bodies tend to require training providers to ensure learners' records are kept for 3 years.

OTHER BENEFITS OF RECORD KEEPING

Learners who have attended a course often require evidence of past attendance on the course. If the records are not kept then there is nothing to show or present to the learner.

REFERENCES

Kolb, D.A and Fry, R. (1975). Toward an applied theory of experiential learning; in C. Cooper (ed). Theories of Group Process, John Wiley. Cited in Eaton, R. (2006) Learning theories and theorists, Dunstable College.

PETTY, G (2004) Teaching Today: A practical Guide, Nelson Thornes.

REECE I, and WALKER S, (1997) Teaching, Training, Training: a practical guide, Business Education Publishers.

www.ingramcontent.com/pod-product-compliance
Lightning Source LLC
Chambersburg PA
CBHW042359070526
44585CB00029B/2990